The edition of *The Complete Works of Frances Ridley Havergal* has five parts:

Volume I   *Behold Your King: The Complete Poetical Works of Frances Ridley Havergal*

Volume II   *Whose I Am and Whom I Serve: Prose Works of Frances Ridley Havergal*

Volume III   *Loving Messages for the Little Ones: Works for Children by Frances Ridley Havergal*

Volume IV   *Love for Love: Frances Ridley Havergal: Memorials, Letters and Biographical Works*

Volume V   *Songs of Truth and Love: Music by Frances Ridley Havergal and William Henry Havergal*

David L. Chalkley, Editor   Dr. Glen T. Wegge, Music Editor

Frances Ridley Havergal's formal education ended when she was 17, with one term at a young women's school in Düsseldorf, Germany, yet she was a true scholar all her life. Fluent in German and French and nearly so in Italian, she read and loved the Reformers in Latin, German, and French. Knowledge was never an end in itself, only a means to know better her Lord and Saviour and to help to bring others to know Him. The Bible was her only Book, and she studied the Hebrew and Greek texts of Scripture, memorized nearly all the New Testament and large portions of the Old Testament, and loved the Author with all her being.

Frances was brought to a saving knowledge of Christ when she was 14, and the rest of her life was consecrated to her Saviour, the Lord Jesus. Keenly aware of her own sinfulness and inability, her sole desire was to please and glorify Him alone. Very finely gifted, she was truly diligent with her gifts: her poetry is among the finest in the English language, after George Herbert; her prose works are deeply beneficial; a musician to the core, she left behind important compositions. Like her works, her life richly touched the ones near her and countless many who met or heard her. The Lord Jesus Christ was her alone, only beauty, and she glowed Him and His truth. Never wanting attention to herself, Frances' desire of her heart was for herself and for others to know her King, the Lord Jesus Christ. Her works are a gold-mine of help and enrichment. There is life in these pages: her works truly glorify the Lord, truly benefit His people, and powerfully reach those who do not yet know Him.

The Music of Frances Ridley Havergal by Glen T. Wegge, Ph.D.

This Companion Volume to the Havergal edition is a valuable presentation of F.R.H.'s scores, most or nearly all of F.R.H.'s scores very little if any at all seen, or even known of, for nearly a century. What a valuable body of music has been unknown for so long and is now made available to many. Dr. Wegge completed his Ph.D. in Music Theory at Indiana University at Bloomington, and his diligence and thoroughness in this volume are obvious. First an analysis of F.R.H.'s compositions is given, an essay that both addresses the most advanced musicians and also reaches those who are untrained in music; then all the extant scores that have been found are newly typeset, with complete texts for each score and extensive indices at the end of the book. This volume presents F.R.H.'s music in newly typeset scores diligently prepared by Dr. Wegge, and Volume V of the Havergal edition presents the scores in facsimile, the original 19th century scores. (The essay—a dissertation—analysing her scores is given the same both in this Companion Volume and in Volume V of the Havergal edition.)

Dr. Wegge is also preparing all of these scores for publication in performance folio editions.

The Havergal Trust   P.O.Box 649   Kirksville, Missouri 63501

No portrait of Charles Henry Purday has been found; if found, his portrait would be placed here with Frances Ridley Havergal's portrait. T[...] portrait was made in Frances' last year, when she was visiting friends in London, in February 1879 (after her 42nd birthday on December 1[...] There are strong reasons to think that this portrait is in no way flattering but gives an accurate copy of how she looked at that time. Ira Sankey, [...] L. Moody's song leader, visited her weeks before her very unexpected early death, and he later commented on how young she looked; others a[...] commented on how she looked younger than her age in years. Both Frances and her family would have accepted only an accurate, realistic, tru[...] ful portrait, never a flattering one. The brooch was a gift to her from her father, having Frances' personal emblem, a harp; this was one of very f[...] pieces of jewelry she kept, clearly special to her, and she had months earlier sold nearly all her other jewelry, to give the proceeds to the suppor[...] foreign missions. She was full of life and love, glowing Christ, and those who knew her or saw and heard her realized what can scarcely be convey[...] on paper. In this way her sister Miriam wrote of how she sang "in quick tune, and with the spirit which only those who heard her can imagi[...] (from the small book *Footprints and Living Songs*, the essay on Frances' hymns by Miriam Crane). Her sister Maria was quoted in the follow[...] notice printed in the newspaper *The Christian* for July 3, 1879: "THE LATE MISS F. RIDLEY HAVERGAL.—Mr. T. J. Hughes, of 2 Elm R[...] Hampstead [London], has shown us a portrait in chalk for which Miss Havergal sat to him several times. This likeness is recommended by her [...] ter, Miss M. V. G. Havergal, as being so life-like. Orders for photographic copies, at a guinea each, may be sent to Mr. Hughes." David Chalk[...]

SONGS OF PEACE AND JOY.

The Music by

Charles H. Purday.

The Words Selected from

The Ministry of Song and *Under the Surface*

Written by

Frances Ridley Havergal.

A Facsimile Copy of the Second Edition Published by James Nisbet & Co., London, 1879

Taken from the New Edition of
The Complete Works of Frances Ridley Havergal.

" Knowing her intense desire that Christ should be magnified, whether
by her life or in her death, may it be to His glory
that in these pages she, being dead,
'Yet speaketh!'"

SONGS OF PEACE AND JOY.
Words by Frances Ridley Havergall set to Music by Charles Henry Purday
Copyright © 2017 by the Havergal Trust.

ISBN 978-1-937236-58-8   Library of Congress Control Number: 2017901561

Printed in the United States of America   *This book is printed on acid-free paper.*

Cover Design by Glen T. Wegge.

Havergal, Frances Ridley and Charles Henry Purday
Songs of Peace and Joy: prose, poetry, and music taken from the edition of the complete works of Frances Ridley Havergal. 1. Havergal, Frances Ridley, 1836–1879, and Charles Henry Purday, 1799–1885. 2. Christian Life. 3. Christian Poetry, English. 4. Music. I. Title

This is taken from *The Complete Works of Frances Ridley Havergal.*
David L. Chalkley, General Editor.   Dr. Glen T. Wegge, Music Editor.

---

633 **(25) ZEAL.**
1 Sam. xii. 24. *" Consider how great things He hath done for you."*
Tune BACA.   6 6 6 6, 6 6.

BACA (Valley of). [H. P. 116.]

1 I GAVE My life for thee,
　My precious blood I shed
That thou might'st ransomed be,
　And quickened from the dead.
I gave My life for thee:
What hast thou given for Me?

2 I spent long years for thee,
　In weariness and woe,
That an eternity
　Of joy thou mightest know.
I spent long years for thee:
Hast thou spent one for Me?

3 My Father's home of light,
　My rainbow-circled throne,
I left, for earthly night,
　For wanderings sad and lone.
I left it all for thee:
Hast thou left aught for Me?

4 I suffered much for thee,
　More than thy tongue may tell
Of bitterest agony,
　To rescue thee from hell.

I suffered much for thee:
What canst thou bear for Me?

5 And I have brought to thee,
　Down from My home above,
Salvation full and free,
　My pardon and My love.
Great gifts I brought to thee:
What hast thou brought to Me?

6 Oh! let thy life be given,
　Thy years for Him be spent,
World-fetters all be riven,
　And joy with suffering blent.
Bring thou thy worthless all:
Follow thy Saviour's call!

Frances Ridley Havergal, 1859.

This is Frances Ridley Havergal's hymn "I gave My life for thee" set to her father's score "Baca," published as number 633 in *Songs Grace and Glory*. Frances wrote in a letter to a friend: "I was so overwhelmed on Sunday at hearing three of my hymns touchingly su at Perry Church. I never before realized the high privilege of writing for 'the great congregation'; especially 633, "I gave My life thee" to papa's tune 'Baca'; the others were 120 and 921 in 'S.G.G.' " (*Memorials of Frances Ridley Havergal* by Maria Vernon Graha Havergal, London: James Nisbet & Co., 1880, original book page 105, page 31 of Volume IV of the Havergal edition) Her sist Maria wrote that this hymn "first appeared in *Good Words.* It was written in Germany, 1858. She had come in weary, and sat dov opposite a picture with this motto. At once the lines flashed upon her, and she wrote them in pencil on a scrap of paper. Readi them over, they did not satisfy her. She tossed them into the fire, but they fell out untouched! Showing them some months after her father, he encouraged her to preserve them, and wrote the tune 'Baca' specially for them." (*Memorials*, original book page 65, pa 21 of Volume IV of the Havergal edition)

For more than six years, Dr. Glen T. Wegge has been involved in the work to complete the Havergal edition. Without payment of money, with remarkable diligence, patience, persistence, and hard work, he has labored to prepare for publication all of the music in the Havergal edition, and also to complete and publish his own book, *The Music of Frances Ridley Havergal*, a Companion Volume to this edition of *The Complete Works of Frances Ridley Havergal*. He has also done so much to bring to completion (in countless hours of work) all of the other books in the Havergal edition. The patience and support of his wife, Denise, are also appreciated. So much thought, diligence, hard work, countless hours, a servant's heart, a labor of love. My estimate or guess is that Glen has worked approximately 1,500 hours on the Havergal edition, without pay. His work is remarkable both in quantity and in quality, first-rate, sterling work. How many times ? (the Lord knows how many times) has he gone back again and again to fix a text or an illustration until it was just right. Most of the details of his work were known only to Glen and me, much now forgotten, but God sees and knows every trace. How compassionately and richly He has blessed us in all of this.

For much or most of the past 100 years, few if any have realized the value of Frances' music, and Glen (who completed his Ph.D. in music theory at Indiana University at Bloomington and is so finely gifted and prepared to do this work) is the first one to analyze and present her music in such a scholarly way. He began his work on this in very difficult circumstances, and his diligence, persistence, and servant's heart are a true example for believers. Glen is worthy of strong gratitude from all those who will be encouraged and enriched by F.R.H.'s poetry, prose, and music.

The Lord reward him as I cannot, as no man can reward.

This is all the Lord's doing. Thanks be to God for His indescribable gift to us in Christ.

David Chalkley

The Complete Works of Frances Ridley Havergal is dedicated to the glory of the Lord Jesus Christ, laying this at His feet and asking Him to bless to others what He has provided,

"for Jesus' sake only"

and is gratefully inscribed to two people:

Miss Janet Grierson,
Mr. Stanley Ward.

Miss Grierson's Biography and her other work on F.R.H. are the most important work on Frances since Maria V. G. Havergal, and she has been invaluably helpful in the preparation of this edition.

Mr. Stanley Ward has been deeply interested in Frances since the 1960's, and his kindness, insights, and help have been truly and profoundly important to this edition.

Thanks be to God for His indescribable gift to us in Christ.

CONTENTS

ILLUSTRATIONS

(To James Parlane.)

1876.

". . . I must tell you a wonderful bit of *Ministry of Song*, through 'Whom having not seen, ye love.' I was taken on speculation to call on a clever young gentleman, just an infidel, knowing the Bible and disbelieving it, and believing that nobody else really believes, but that religion is all humbug and mere profession. I was not primed at all, only knew that he was 'not a religious man.' In the first place, I had no end of fun with him, and got on thoroughly good terms—then was asked to sing. I prayed the whole time I was singing, and *felt* God very near and helping me. After a Handel song or two which greatly delighted him, I sang 'Tell it out!' felt the glorious truth that He *is* King, and couldn't help breaking off in the very middle and *saying* so, right out!

"Then I sang, 'Whom having not seen, ye love,' and felt as if I could sing out all the love of my heart in it. Well, this young infidel, who had seemed extremely surprised and subdued by 'Tell it out,' completely broke down, and went away to hide his tears in a bay window. And afterwards we sat down together, and he let me 'tell it out' as I pleased, and it was not hard to speak of Him of whom I had sung. He seemed altogether struck and subdued, and listened like a child. He said, 'Well there *is* faith then, *you* have it anyhow—I saw it when you sang, and I could not stand it, and that's the fact!' He was anxious for me to come again.

"When I came away, his sister, who had introduced me, wept for joy, saying she had persuaded me to come with a vague hope that he '*might* find he could tolerate a religious person,' but never dared to hope such an effect as this, and that she thought I had been most marvellously guided in drawing the bow at a venture, for every word and even action had been just right. I tell you this just because you are publishing both 'Tell it out' and other leaflets for me. Will you sometimes pray that God's especial blessing will go with them? I should add that it was almost a miracle in another way, for I had such a wretched cold that I doubted being able to sing *at all*, and yet I believe I never sang clearer and better and stronger. How *good* God is!"[1]

During a previous visit to London, Frances was invited to an amateur musical evening. Some classical music was rendered, and F. was especially riveted by the finished singing of an Italian lady. Presently my sister was invited, last of all, to the piano. True to her resolve, 'Let me sing only, always, for my King,' she chose a song of Handel's. Then the hostess gracefully pressed for one of her own compositions, so she sang, 'Whom having not seen ye love.' She always sang so rejoicingly the words, 'Though now ye see Him not, yet believing ye rejoice,' up the scale of joy—she knows better now—and then the deep adoring thrill, 'With joy unspeakable and full of glory.' The rooms were hushed, and then the Italian stranger, with tears in her eyes, sought her as she left the piano, 'Miss Havergal, I envy you; your words and face tell me you have something I have not.' "[2]

---

[1] Maria Havergal, editor, *Letters*, pp. 265–266. See Volume IV of the Havergal edition, pp. 221–222.
[2] Maria Havergal, *Autobiography*, pp. 81–82. See Volume IV of the Havergal edition, pp. 513–514.

PREFACE

Songs of Peace and Joy (words by Frances Ridley Havergal, music by Charles Henry Purday) was published by James Nisbet & Co., London, in 1879. Charles H. Purday, over 80 when this volume of music was completed, was a composer whose music William Henry Havergal had admired. A finely gifted singer, he had sung at the coronation of Queen Victoria in 1838 when F.R.H. was a toddler. In the summer of 1878 he for the first time read poems by F.R.H. in *The Ministry of Song* and *Under the Surface*, and began setting a number of them to music. He wrote to F.R.H., asking her approval, and later she made notes and suggestions to the manuscript scores, gratefully endorsing her senior colleague's work. This has 36 poems by her, nearly all the scores composed by Purday, with two scores by her. Frances' Prefatory Note was signed May 13, 1879, three weeks before her unexpected early death at age 42. Purday's Composer's Preface was signed October 1, 1879.

Charles Henry Purday (January 11, 1799 to April 23, 1885) "was appointed conductor of psalmody at Crown Court Scots Church in Covent Garden, London , in the 1840's, during the ministry of Dr. John Cumming. Dr. Cumming's church was so popular that it was said traffic could not move in Bow Street and Drury Lane for the throng of carriages making their way to services. He became a music publisher, and was a pioneer in the movement for copyright law reform. His works include *The Sacred Musical Offering*, 1833; *Crown Court Psalmody: One Hundred Psalm Tunes and Chants*, 1854; *A Few Directions for Chanting*, 1855; *A Church and Home Tune Book*, 1857; and *Copyright, a Sketch of Its Rise and Progress*, 1877." (*Historical Companion to Hymns Ancient & Modern* edited by Maurice Frost, London, William Clowes & Sons, Ltd., 1962, page 687)

Maria in her *Memorials* of F.R.H. mentioned this briefly, writing this:

> "She was interested in looking over some musical settings to her words by Mr. Purday, an old correspondent of our father's. She approved of the title, "Songs of Peace and Joy"; and against some of his tunes wrote "very sweet," "very good," "fair, third strain interesting," etc. [1]

F.R.H. wrote these next four letters or excerpts of letters to C. H. Purday. [2]

(To the late C. H. Purday.)

The Mumbles, October 14, 1878.

Your note has touched and interested me most deeply. "Heart answereth to heart." I do trust that ere now you are still further on the way to recovery. Yet there is, I know, so much real blessing in the touch of our Lord's hand, even when we have to say, "Thy hand presseth me sore," that somehow, ever since a very long and suffering illness of my own, I have hardly been able to say sincerely to any really Christian friend, "I am sorry you have been ill." And the "afterward" is surely promised. Every time of calling apart leads us to know and understand a little better "Him with whom we have to do." How much these words imply! . . .

I am so glad you like my *Royal Commandments*, though I should not have expected you to like it so well as *Royal Bounty*. Mr. Snepp is charmed with your tune to "Yes, He knows the way is dreary," and would be very glad to include it in his new edition.

Possibly the enclosed tiny books may give you some pleasant thought—I shall be so thankful if they do. (Precious Things, and I also for thee.) [3]

(To the same.)

The Mumbles, October 30, 1878.

. . . I am so glad to hear you are raised up again. It is curious that in the night I was thinking so much of the promise, "Thou shalt glorify Me," specially in its connection as following deliverance from trouble (Psalm 50:15). And then your letter came in the morning, speaking of your desire to do something for His glory! Whatever He has promised, surely we may and should claim and expect, however much better and greater it may be than we should have thought of asking. Oh yes, if one may but do anything for Him "who loved us and washed us from our sins in His own blood," it is worth coming back from the very golden gates to do it. If He has made us for His glory He will surely "be glorified in us." That He will even now, and there is 2 Thessalonians 1:10 to come! It is so wonderful.

---

[1] *Memorials of Frances Ridley Havergal* by her sister Maria Vernon Graham Havergal (London: James Nisbet & Co., 1880, page 284). See page 81 of Volume IV of the Havergal edition.

[2] *Letters by the Late Frances Ridley Havergal* edited by her sister Maria V. G. Havergal (London: James Nisbet & Co., 1886), pages 308–312 and 330–331. See pages 233–234 and 239–240 of Volume IV of the Havergal edition.

[3] "Precious Things" and "I also . . . . for thee" were two pamphlets or "penny books" by F. R.H. In the line of the address and date at the top of the letters here, the Mumbles was a village near Swansea, Wales, where Frances lived the last eight months of her life.

(To the late C. H. Purday.)

December 30, 1878.

I have been on the shelf, or should have replied sooner. And now the few days' illness has thrown me all behind with letters and work, so pardon haste. The only tune I do not like, and cannot possibly sanction, in your *Songs of Peace and Joy*, is the setting of my Consecration hymn, "Take my life," to that wearisomely hackneyed kyrie of Mozart. It does not suit the words either, and I was much vexed with Mr. Mountain for printing it with it in his *Hymns of Consecration*, and it would just spoil your book to let it pass. I particularly wish that hymn kept to my dear father's sweet little tune, "Patmos," which suits it perfectly. So please substitute that, and your book will be the gainer. You have rather taken the wind out of my own sails by your book, as Hutchings & Romer have for a good while wanted me to set *Loyal Responses* to music (now published by them); but I have so many irons in the fire, that I can barely find time to heat a musical one. However, I could not find it in my heart to hinder you in your wish, with which my whole heart sympathizes, to do this thing for God's glory. I do so very much like many of your tunes.

"Therefore, being justified by faith, we have peace with God." Dear friend, why say, "May that peace be mine," when it is yours already, purchased for you, made for you, sealed for you, pledged to you—by the word of the Father and the "precious blood of Jesus"! Forgive me for touching up your words, but I have recalled them so many times since you wrote.

(F. R. H. to C. H. Purday.)

May 1, 1879.

Glad it is all straight now for Nisbet! Shall leave form and style and everything to you and Mr. N.

Thanks, I rarely have anything the matter with me except what arises from over-pressure. God has given me an exceptionally healthy set of organs, so all doctors tell me, only they add, "Your physique is not equal to the brain and nerves." "If you could live as an oyster, you might be a little Hercules," said one to me! But I cannot live as an oyster! I have always more to write and do and talk and attend to than I can get through in the day without just so much fatigue and pressure as keeps me nearly always more or less suffering or exhausted. It is the little things that do it—"only just" this note and that letter, and the other ten minutes' interview, and so on—all day long! And I cannot live near a poor village (Newton Mumbles) and not get doing anything for the people—and one thing always involves and leads on to another, and the very success that God gives to really everything I put my hand to, wears me out. A special branch of work for the Irish Society, which I started only two years ago, thinking merely to have about a dozen juvenile collectors in tow, forthwith grew, so that there are now more than 100, all in my own hands, and this will ere long be multiplied and be kept organized with lots of other things growing out of it. I only name this as one out of many similar growths, and your kind interest deserved an explanation of the state of things once for all! Then every time I pay a visit, I always get a whole following of fresh friends, and readers and correspondents! I can't imagine where into it will grow! And sometimes I look longingly to the land that is very far away just for rest.

The Consecration Hymn, "Take my life"

F.R.H. wrote this hymn on February 4, 1874. She wrote a fair copy autograph of this on pages 14–15 of her Manuscript Book Nº VIII, and facsimile copies of these two manuscript pages are found on page xv after these comments. At the top of her fair copy autograph she wrote, "Yea, let him take all!" (a quotation of part of II Samuel 19:30). Her fair copy autograph in 1874 differs in details from her finalized poem which she published in *Loyal Responses* in 1878, and the words of the original *Loyal Responses* (with words only—full of music but without written notes) are definitive. In her handwritten "Index" near the end of this Manuscript Book Nº VIII, she listed this with the name "Consecration Hymn,"

and this name has been used for this hymn since then. Though published previously in leaflets or periodicals, she published this as the First Day of *Loyal Responses* in 1878, and between the title "Consecration Hymn" and the first verse, she gave this quotation from the Anglican *Book of Common Prayer*: "Here we offer and present unto Thee, O Lord, ourselves, our souls and bodies, to be a reasonable, holy, and lively sacrifice unto Thee."

Frances clearly wanted the Consecration Hymn to be sung to her father's hymn score "Patmos," and she wrote this statement in a letter to Charles Henry Purday on December 30, 1878: "I *particularly wish* that hymn ["Take my life"] kept to my dear father's sweet little tune, 'Patmos,' which suits it perfectly."[1]

She wrote this in a letter to a friend:

> Perhaps you will be interested to know the origin of the Consecration hymn, "Take my life." I went for a little visit of five days. There were ten persons in the house, some unconverted and long prayed for, some converted but not rejoicing Christians. He gave me the prayer, "Lord, give me *all* in this house!" And He just *did!* Before I left the house every one had got a blessing. The last night of my visit I was too happy to sleep, and passed most of the night in praise and renewal of my own consecration, and these little couplets formed themselves and chimed in my heart one after another, till they finished with, "*Ever*, ONLY, ALL for Thee!"[2]

In her sister Maria's biography of her, after that quotation, Maria soon quoted Frances from another place:

> Let us sing words which we feel and love, sacrificing everything to clearness of enunciation,[3] and looking up to meet His smile all the while we are singing; our songs will reach more hearts than those of finer voices and more brilliant execution, unaccompanied by His power. A sacred song thus sung often gives a higher tone to the

---

[1] *Letters by the Late Frances Ridley Havergal* edited by her sister Maria Vernon Graham Havergal (London: James Nisbet & Co., 1885), original book page 311, page 234 of Volume IV of the Havergal edition.

[2] *Memorials of Frances Ridley Havergal* by Maria V. G. Havergal (London: James Nisbet & Co., 1880), original book pages 132–133, page 37 of Volume IV of this edition. Miss Janet Grierson wrote that this was a visit to Areley House (near Stourport, a small city on the River Severn in Worcestershire), the home of Joseph Rogers and his family, relatives of Frances' sister's husband, Henry Crane (on page 1247 of Volume IV, in Chapter 12 of Miss Grierson's book *Singing for Jesus*, published for the first time in Volume IV of this edition. Chapter 12 of *Singing for Jesus* by Miss Grierson has valuable details on this hymn. See also page 1200 of Volume IV of this edition.

[3] This is very important. The true priority should be clarity of communication, that the hearers be able to understand the words and the truth of the words. Both speaking and singing should be to serve, help, benefit others, to show them truth, never to seek to impress anyone with our ability nor to want the praise of men: to help hearers to see Christ, His truth, His glory, never to parade nor magnify ourselves; to point hearers to Him, never to ourselves. Both in speaking and in singing, for individuals and for choirs, there should never be any false "art" that renders unclear the words. The clear communication of truth to needing ones is so great, and will be the priority of true love. I Corinthians 14:19 The New Testament was not written in the Classical Greek of scholars, which many might not be able to follow or understand fully, but in the Koine Greek of the common people, language that dishwashers, laborers, anyone, could understand. The truth of Christ, and the great need of sinners (also the need of believers to understand truth communicated), is so extremely important, and true love will seek to make that truth clear to see, understand and follow. See also F.R.H.'s letter to James Parlane, so valuable, on page ix of this book. This is true love as the two commandments say (Matthew 22:37–40), which only the Lord Jesus Christ alone can do in a person. D.C.

evening, and affords, both to singer and listeners, some opportunity of speaking a word for Jesus.

. . . . I was at a large regular London party lately, and I was so happy. He seemed to give me "the secret of His presence," and of course I sang "for Jesus," and did not I have dead silence? Afterwards I had two really important conversations with strangers; one seemed extremely surprised at finding himself *quite easily* drifted from the badinage with which he started into a right-down personal talk about *his* personal danger and *his* only hope for safety; he took it very well, and thanked me. Perhaps that seed may bear fruit. Somehow it is wonderful how the Master manages for me in such cases. I don't think any one can say I force the subject; it just all develops one thing out of another, quite naturally, till very soon they find themselves face to face with eternal things, and the Lord Jesus can be freely "lifted up" before them. I could not *contrive* a conversation thus.[4]

On December 2, 1873, Frances read a pamphlet by Dr. John Tinson Wrenford entitled "All for Jesus," and this pamphlet and a letter by Wrenford to her, in which he wrote about I John 1:7, very profoundly moved and benefitted her. Again, Maria in her *Memorials* quoted Frances:

Yes, it was on Advent Sunday, December 2nd, 1873, I first saw it as a flash of electric light, and what you *see* you can never *unsee*. There must be full surrender before there can be full blessedness. God admits you by the one into the other. He Himself showed me all this most clearly. You know how singularly I have been withheld from attending all conventions and conferences; man's teaching has, consequently, had but little to do with it. First, I was shown that "the blood of Jesus Christ His Son cleanseth us from all sin," and then it was made plain to me that He who had thus cleansed me had power to keep me clean; so I just utterly yielded myself to Him, and utterly trusted Him to keep me.[5]

Wrenford's pamphlet and his letter to her were a source or origin of the Consecration Hymn. Clear in her mind was that full surrender and consecration to Christ meant His keeping of what is committed to Him, and our trusting Him to keep us. On the fifth anniversary of that date, December 2, 1878, she wrote this to Wrenford:

I had a great time early this morning, renewing the never regretted consecration. I seemed led to run over the "Take my life," and could bless Him verse by verse for having led me on to much more definite consecration than even when I wrote it, voice, gold, intellect, etc.[6]

Maria wrote this account:

My dear sister Frances went to Swansea on Thursday, 17th. I sent our good maid M. Farrington with her, as she did not wish me to go; she says that on the way Miss Frances talked so humbly, and that she "felt as if she had no right to go teaching others—such a sinner as I am; but then Mary, I am just trusting for every word." The room was quite full. Mrs. Morgan, not knowing F.'s subject, had chosen a hymn that did not suit it, and my sister always thought it important that hymns should be suitably chosen. As her subject for the evening was from Hosea 3, "I also for thee," (see *Starlight Through the Shadows*), F. said she wished to sing "Precious Saviour, may I live, only for Thee." Mrs. Morgan said they did not know her tune to it ("Onesimus," *S.G.G.* 257 [hymn 257 in *Songs of Grace and Glory*].) F.: "No fear! Do let me just sing one verse alone, and I know they will join." Going to the piano and turning her face to them, she sang with her own bright ringing cheeriness one verse, and then all joined most heartily with her. Mary told me of my sister's soft pleading voice—that her words were intensely tender and entreating. At the close of the meeting, my sister gave to each one a card with her Consecration hymn, "Take my life and let it be Consecrated, Lord, to Thee," specially prepared and printed for this evening (Messrs. Parlane, Paisley, still supply them). Her own name was omitted, and a blank space left for signature. As she gave the cards, she

---

[4] *Memorials*, original book pages 133–134, pages 37–38 of Volume IV.

[5] *Memorials*, original book pages 126–127, page 36 of Volume IV. Though not fully quoted here, all the details on page 36 of Volume IV are truly valuable. The Scripture that Frances quoted is I John 1:7.

[6] *Memorials*, original book page 269, page 71 of Volume IV.

asked them to make that hymn a test before God, and if they could really do so, to sign it on their knees at home. Then the hymn was sung to our dear father's tune "Patmos" (No. 145, *S.G.G.*).

It seems to have been a great night of decision to many present. The next morning, before ever her breakfast was finished, one and another came for conversation with my dear sister—a French governess was specially impressed. My sister returned very much exhausted—meetings seemed to take away her little physical strength, and yet she always cheerfully took up any work for her King.[7]

Her last completed book,[8] *Kept for the Master's Use*, was based on the Consecration Hymn, an enlargement and rich presentation of the truths in those twelve couplets.

Another title that has been used for this hymn is "All for Jesus," a title not given by Frances, though she would have surely agreed with the title. Is *all* given, committed, entrusted, to Him? and is all the work His doing, His keeping, His using, none of our own doing but His doing alone? John 15:5, Philippians 4:13, Romans 7:18, I Corinthians 15:10, II Timothy 1:12

David L. Chalkle

This is the finalized text that F.R.H. published as the First Day of *Loyal Responses* in 1878:

Consecration Hymn.

"Here we offer and present unto Thee, O Lord, ourselves, our souls
and bodies, to be a reasonable, holy, and lively sacrifice unto Thee."

Take my life, and let it be
Consecrated, Lord, to Thee.

Take my moments and my days;
Let them flow in ceaseless praise.

Take my hands, and let them move
At the impulse of Thy love.

Take my feet, and let them be
Swift and "beautiful" for Thee.

Take my voice, and let me sing
Always, only, for my King.

Take my lips, and let them be
Filled with messages from Thee.

Take my silver and my gold;
Not a mite would I withhold.

Take my intellect, and use
Every power as Thou shalt choose.

Take my will, and make it Thine;
It shall be no longer mine.

Take my heart, it *is* Thine own;
It shall be Thy royal throne.

Take my love; my Lord, I pour
At Thy feet its treasure-store.

Take myself, and I will be
Ever, *only*, ALL for Thee.

Frances Ridley Havergal

---

7 *Letters by the Late Frances Ridley Havergal*, original book pages 326–327, page 238 of Volume IV. This was a "Memorandum" by Maria in *Letters by t* *Late Frances Ridley Havergal*. (This was April 17, 1879, 47 days before Frances died.)

8 *Kept for the Master's Use* by F.R.H. (London: James Nisbet & Co., 1879), on pages 417–500 of Volume II of this edition. In the "Prefatory Note" to th book, Maria wrote that Frances "finished revising the proofs of this book shortly before her death on Whit Tuesday, June 3, 1879."

This is F.R.H.'s fair copy autograph of the Consecration Hymn in her Manuscript Book Nº VIII. Note that there are small differences in this manuscript and the finalized text published by F.R.H. The title was named "Consecration Hymn." The seventh couplet (beginning "Take my moments") was moved to be the second couplet, and in line 2 of the eighth couplet, "dost" was changed to "shalt." These changes were made by Frances herself, before she published this as the First Day in Loyal Responses.

STAY AND THINK.

Words and Music by
Frances Ridley Havergal

Lyrics under the music:

1. Know-ing that the God on high, With a ten-der Fa-ther's grace, Waits to hear your faint-est cry, Waits to show a Fa-ther's face:— Stay and Think! Stay and Think! Stay and Think! Stay and Think! How He loves!—Oh, should not— you Love this gra-ciousFa-ther too?

2. Knowing Christ was crucified,
   Knowing that He loves you now
Just as much as when He died
   With the thorns upon His brow,—
   Stay and think!—
How He loves! oh, should not you
Love this blessèd Saviour too?

3. Knowing that a Spirit strives
   With your weary, wandering heart,
Who can change the restless lives,
   Pure and perfect peace impart,—
   Stay and think!—
How He loves! oh, should not you
Love this loving Spirit too?

TRUST.

223

FIDES.   [H. P. 343.]

HERMAS.*   [H. P. 105.]

569   Ps. lv. 23. *"I will trust in Thee."*
Tune FIDES. 65, 65. D.   Or HERMAS.

1 JESUS, I will trust Thee, trust Thee with my soul;
    Guilty, lost, and helpless, Thou canst make me whole.
There is none in heaven or on earth like Thee:
Thou hast died for sinners—therefore, Lord, for me.

2 Jesus, I may trust Thee, name of matchless
        worth
Spoken by the angel at Thy wondrous birth;
Written, and for ever, on Thy cross of shame,
Sinners read and worship, trusting in that
    name.

3 Jesus, I must trust Thee, pondering Thy ways,
Full of love and mercy all Thine earthly days:
Sinners gathered round Thee, lepers sought
        Thy face—
None too vile or loathsome for a Saviour's grace.

4 Jesus, I can trust Thee, trust Thy written word,
Though Thy voice of pity I have never heard.
When Thy Spirit teacheth, to my taste **how**
    sweet—
Only may I hearken, sitting at Thy feet.

5 Jesus, I do trust Thee, trust without a doubt:
"Whosoever cometh, Thou wilt not cast out,"
Faithful is Thy promise, precious is Thy blood—
These my soul's salvation, Thou my Saviour
        God!
                            Mary Jane Walker, 1864.

See Hymns 1076—1078.

* To this tune its composer, FRANCES RIDLEY HAVERGAL, sang
the first verse of this hymn ten minutes only before her death,
Tuesday morning, June 3, 1879.

This is a copy of the top two-thirds of page 223 in *Songs of Grace and Glory* (the "New and Enlarged Musical Edition," London: James Nisbet & Co., 1880), the most comprehensive hymnbook till that time in the Church of England, edited by Rev. Charles Busbridge Snepp (texts) and Frances Ridley Havergal (music). Read the asterisked note by Rev. Snepp in this edition after her death: " * To this tune [Hermas] its composer, Frances Ridley Havergal, sang the first verse of this hymn ten minutes only before her death, Thursday morning, June 3, 1879." See also pages 62–63 of this book.

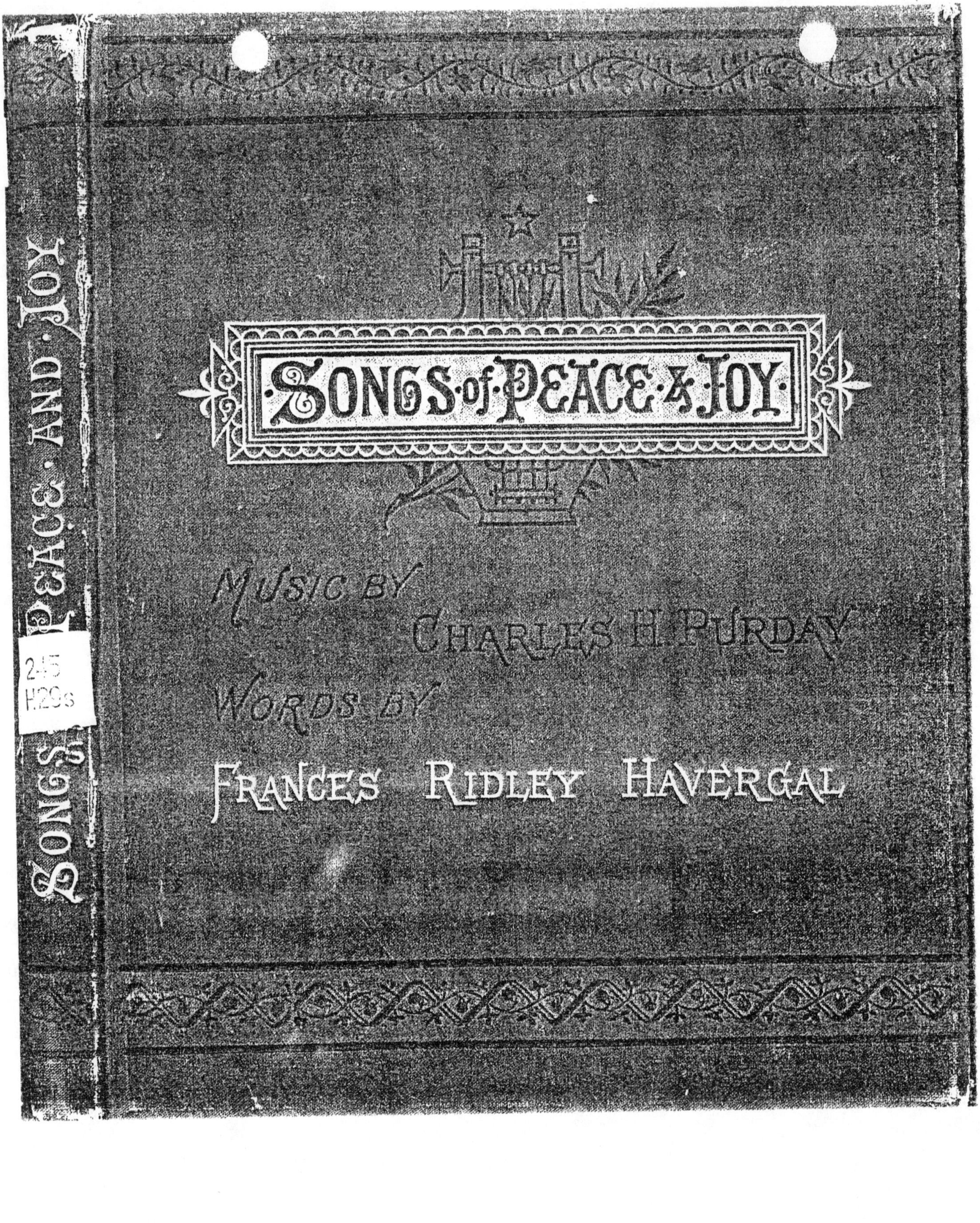
SONGS·of·PEACE·&·JOY
MUSIC BY
CHARLES H. PURDAY
WORDS BY
FRANCES RIDLEY HAVERGAL
SONGS OF PEACE · AND · JOY
245
H29s

Songs of Peace and Joy.

THE MUSIC BY

CHARLES H. PURDAY.

THE WORDS SELECTED FROM

"THE MINISTRY OF SONG" *and* "UNDER THE SURFACE,"

WRITTEN BY

FRANCES RIDLEY HAVERGAL.

SECOND EDITION.

London:

JAMES NISBET & CO., 21, BERNERS STREET, W.

WEEKES & CO., 16, HANOVER STREET, W.

1879.

Singing for Jesus.

Singing for Jesus, our Saviour & King,
 Singing for Jesus, the Lord whom we love!
All adoration we joyously bring,
 Longing to praise as they praise Him above.

Singing for Jesus, our Master & Friend,
 Telling His love & His marvellous grace,
Love from eternity, love without end,
 Love for the loveless, the sinful, & base.

Singing for Jesus, and trying to win
 Many to love Him & join in the song;
Calling the weary and wandering in,
 Rolling the chorus of gladness along.

Singing for Jesus, our Life & our Light,
Singing for Him as we press to the mark;
Singing for Him when the morning is bright,
Singing, still singing, for Him in the dark!

Singing for Jesus, our Shepherd & Guide,

 Singing for gladness of heart that He gives;
Singing for wonder & praise that He died,
 Singing for blessing & joy that He lives.

Singing for Jesus, oh singing with joy!
 Thus will we praise Him, & tell out His love,
Till He shall call us to brighter employ,
 Singing for Jesus for ever above.

June 12.

F.R.H.'s fair copy autograph of "Singing for Jesus" in her Manuscript Book Nº VI. She wrote this on June 12, 1872. See pages 18–19 of this book.

Note: This was a blank page in the original book.

PREFATORY NOTE.

———

THIS little book contains upwards of Thirty musical settings of selected verses from

"THE MINISTRY OF SONG" and "UNDER THE SURFACE."

It may be interesting to mention that, with the exception of three or four, they are the production of an octogenarian friend, whose desire is that his work may be to the glory of that faithful God who has led him for more than twice forty years through the wilderness; and that his chosen title for these little melodies,

"SONGS OF PEACE AND JOY,"

may be true of the experience of all who shall sing them.

FRANCES RIDLEY HAVERGAL.

May 13, 1879.

A Worker's Prayer.

Tune—CASWELL BAY.

Words and Music by
F. R. HAVERGAL.

Lord, speak to me, that I may speak In living echoes of Thy tone;

As Thou hast sought, so let me seek Thy erring children, lost and lone.

O lead me, Lord, that I may lead
The wandering and the wavering feet;
O feed me, Lord, that I may feed
Thy hungering ones with manna sweet.

O strengthen me, that while I stand
Firm on the Rock, and strong in Thee,
I may stretch out a loving hand
To wrestlers with the troubled sea.

O teach me, Lord, that I may teach
The precious things Thou dost impart:
And wing my words, that they may reach
The hidden depths of many a heart.

O give Thine own sweet rest to me,
That I may speak with soothing power
A word in season, as from Thee,
To weary ones in needful hour.

O fill me with Thy fulness, Lord,
Until my very heart o'erflow
In kindling thought and glowing word,
Thy love to tell, Thy praise to show.

O use me, Lord, use even me,
Just *as* Thou wilt, and *when*, and *where*,
Until Thy blessed Face I see,
Thy rest, Thy joy, Thy glory share.

1/6 per 100.]   J. & R. Parlane, Paisley

J. & R. Parlane, Paisley, published a number of F.R.H.'s poems with and without her music in leaflets. She composed this score late in her life, her setting of "Just when Thou wilt," the end of the 31 Days of Loyal Responses, and later (apparently posthumously) the score was named "Caswell Bay," where she lived her last eight months and died. In Songs of Grace and Glory, F.R.H. had set this poem to Lowell Mason's "Boston."

Note: This was another blank page in the original book.

COMPOSER'S PREFACE.

IN publishing this little volume, I desire to say that I had never read any of Miss Havergal's beautiful Poems until the summer of 1878, when I was so charmed with the natural flow, lyrical aptitude, and truly Christian sentiments of her poetry, that I felt an intense desire to set some of her Hymns to music. I accordingly wrote to ask her permission to do so, which she readily and most kindly granted, by a short note to me dated August 10, 1878. I then set three of them, which I sent for her approval—viz., "Ministry of Song," v. i and ii, "Be not Weary," and "Wait patiently for Him,"—when she replied, August 24, 1878: "Some of the Hymns have been set already; it would save possible disappointment if you would say beforehand which you would like to set. . . . . Your name is so well known to me, and was so honoured by my dear father, that I am specially gratified at your music and my little words being linked together. May our God grant his special blessing on your plan." Thus encouraged, I went on adapting and occasionally sending her my tunes until they had reached about thirty, corresponding with her at intervals, until it became necessary that we should determine how they should be published. This suggested an interview, and an invitation was sent me to go to Wales for the purpose of going through the M.S. together. "Man proposes, but God disposes," and it was ordered otherwise. Consequently a request was made that I should send the M.S. down, as Miss H. said she could look it over then, and return it before she went on her projected tour to her Irish mission. This was done and the M.S. returned with copious notes and valuable suggestions, to which I had much pleasure in giving effect,—when it pleased the Disposer of all events to call her hence,—how gloriously prepared has been fully stated.* And I have reason to bless God for my acquaintance with her and her works.

C. H. P.

Oct. 1, 1879.   * "The Last Week."

INDEX.

—

Those marked with a star, thus, *, are specially suitable for Congregational Use, or Public Occasions.

Jesus only.

MATT. xvii. 8.

mf

1. 'Je - sus on - ly!' In the sha - dow Of the cloud so
2. 'Je - sus on - ly!' In the glo - ry, When the sha - dows

chill and dim, We are cling - ing, lov - ing, trust - ing
all are flown, See - ing Him in all His beau - ty

He with us, and we with Him; All un - seen, though
Sa - tis - fied with Him a - lone; May we join His

ev - er nigh, 'Je - sus on - ly'— all our cry.
ran - somed throng, 'Je - sus on - ly'— all our song.

(7)

Whose I am.

ACTS xxvii. 23.

Je - sus, Mas - ter, whose I am, Pur -chased Thine a -
- lone to be, By Thy blood, O spot - less Lamb,
Shed so will - ing - ly for me; Let my heart be
all Thine own, Let me live to Thee a - lone.

Jesus, Master, whose I am,
  Purchased Thine alone to be,
By Thy blood, O spotless Lamb,
  Shed so willingly for me;
Let my heart be all Thine own,
Let me live to Thee alone.

Other lords have long held sway,
  Now, Thy name alone to bear,
Thy dear voice alone obey,
  Is my daily, hourly prayer.
Whom have I in heaven but Thee?
Nothing else my joy can be.

Jesus, Master! I am Thine;
  Keep me faithful, keep me near;
Let Thy presence in me shine,
  All my homeward way to cheer.
Jesus! at Thy feet I fall,
Oh, be Thou my All-in-All.

Whom I serve.

ACTS xxvii. 23.

Je - sus, Mas - ter, whom I serve, Though so fee - bly
and so ill, Strength - en hand and heart and nerve,
All Thy bid - ding to ful - fil; O - pen Thou mine
eyes to see All the work Thou hast for me.

Jesus, Master, whom I serve,
  Though so feebly and so ill,
Strengthen hand and heart and nerve,
  All Thy bidding to fulfil;
Open Thou mine eyes to see
All the work Thou hast for me.

Lord, Thou needest not, I know,
  Service such as I can bring,
Yet I long to prove and show
  Full allegiance to my King.
Thou an honour* art to me,
Let me be a praise to Thee.

Jesus, Master, wilt Thou use
  One who owes Thee more than all?
As thou wilt! I would not choose,
  Only let me hear Thy call.
Jesus! let me always be
In Thy service glad and free.

* See marginal reading of 1 Peter ii. 7.

Daily Strength.

DEUT. xxxiii. 25.

'As thy day thy strength shall be,'

This should be e - nough for thee; He who knows thy

frame will spare Bur - dens more than thou canst bear.

'As thy day thy strength shall be,'
This should be enough for thee;
He who knows thy frame will spare
Burdens more than thou canst bear.

When thy days are veiled in night,
Christ shall give thee heavenly light;
Seem they wearisome and long,
Yet in Him thou shalt be strong.

Cold and wintry though they prove,
Thine the sunshine of His love;
Or, with fervid heat oppressed,
In His shadow thou shalt rest.

When thy days on earth are past,
Christ shall call thee home at last,
His redeeming love to praise,
Who hath strengthened all thy days.

Master, say on.

I SAM. iii. 9.

Master, speak! Thy ser - vant hear - eth, Wait - ing
for Thy gra - cious word, Long - ing for Thy voice that cheer - eth;
Mas - ter, let it now be heard. I am
list -'ning, Lord, for Thee; What hast Thou to say to me?

Master, speak! Thy servant heareth,
  Waiting for Thy gracious word,
Longing for Thy voice that cheereth;
  Master, let it now be heard.
I am listening, Lord, for Thee;
What hast Thou to say to me?

Often through my heart is pealing
  Many another voice than Thine,
Many an unwilled echo stealing
  From the walls of this Thy shrine.
Let Thy longed-for accents fall;
Master, speak! and silence all.

Master, speak! I do not doubt Thee,
  Though so tearfully I plead;
Saviour, Shepherd! oh, without Thee
  Life would be a blank indeed.
But I long for fuller light,
Deeper love, and clearer sight.

Master, speak! I kneel before Thee,
  Listening, longing, waiting still;
Oh! how long shall I implore Thee
  This petition to fulfil!
Hast Thou not one word for me?
Must my prayer unanswered be?

Speak to me by name, O Master,
  Let me *know* it is to me;
Speak, that I may follow faster,
  With a step more firm and free,
Where the Shepherd leads the flock,
In the shadow of the rock!

Master, speak! and make me ready,
  When Thy voice is truly heard,
With obedience, glad and steady,
  Still to follow every word.
I am listening, Lord, for Thee;
Master, speak! oh, speak to me!

Singing for Jesus.

Ps. xxviii. 7.

Sing - ing for Je - sus, our Sa - viour and King,

Sing - ing for Je - sus, the Lord whom we love;

All a - do - ra - tion we joy - ous - ly bring,

Long - ing to praise as they praise Him a - bove.

Singing for Jesus, our Saviour and King,
    Singing for Jesus, the Lord whom we love;
All adoration we joyously bring,
    Longing to praise as they praise Him above.

Singing for Jesus, our Master and Friend,
    Telling His love and His marvellous grace;
Love from eternity, love to the end,
    Love for the loveless, the sinful and base.

Singing for Jesus, and trying to win
    Many to love Him, and join in the song;
Calling the weary and wandering in,
    Rolling the chorus of gladness along.

Singing for Jesus, our Life and our Light;
    Singing for Him as we press to the mark;
Singing for Him when the morning is bright;
    Singing, still singing, for Him in the dark.

Singing for Jesus, our Shepherd and Guide,
    Singing for gladness of heart that He gives;
Singing for wonder and praise that He died,
    Singing for blessing and joy that He lives.

Singing for Jesus, oh, singing for joy!
    Thus will we praise Him and tell out His love,
Till He shall call us to brighter employ,
    Singing for Jesus for ever above.

Not your own.

1 Cor. vi. 19.

'Not your own,' but His ye are, Who hath paid a price un - told

For your life, ex-ceed-ing far All earth's store of gems and gold;

With the pre-cious blood of Christ, Ran-som trea-sure all un-priced,

Full re-demp-tion is pro-cured, Full sal - va-tion is as-sured.

'Not your own,' but His ye are,
Who hath paid a price untold
For your life, exceeding far
All earth's store of gems and gold.
With the precious blood of Christ,
Ransom treasure all unpriced,
Full redemption is procured,
Full salvation is assured.

'Not your own,' but His by right,
His peculiar treasure now,
Fair and precious in His sight,
Purchased jewels for His brow!
He will keep what thus He sought,
Safely guard the dearly bought,
Cherish that which He did choose,
Always love, and never lose.

'Not your own,' but His, the King,
His, the Lord of earth and sky,
His, to whom archangels bring
Homage deep and praises high.
What can royal birth bestow?
Or the proudest titles show?
Can such dignity be known
As the glorious name, 'His own'?

'Not your own,' to Him ye owe
All your life and all your love;
Live, that ye His praise may show,
Who is yet all praise above.
Every day and every hour,
Every gift and every power,
Consecrate to Him alone,
Who hath claimed you for His own.

Teach us, Master, how to give
All we have and are to Thee;
Grant us, Saviour, while we live,
Wholly, only, Thine to be.
Henceforth be our calling high,
Thee to serve and glorify;
Ours no longer, but Thine own,
Thine for ever, Thine alone.

Now I see.

JOHN ix. 25.

'Now I see!' But not the part-ing Of the melt-ing earth and sky,

Not a vis-ion dread and startling, Forc-ing one de-spair-ing cry:

But I see the sol-emn say-ing, 'All have sinned, and all must die;

Ho-ly pre-cepts dis-o-bey-ing, Guil-ty all the world must lie.'

Bend-ing, si-lenced, to the dust, Now I see that God is just.

'Now I see!' But not the parting
  Of the melting earth and sky,
Not a vision dread and startling,
  Forcing one despairing cry:
But I see the solemn saying,
  'All have sinned, and all must die;
Holy precepts disobeying,
  Guilty all the world must lie.'
Bending, silenced, to the dust,
Now I see that God is just.

'Now I see!' But not the glory,
  Not the face of Him I love,
Not the full and burning story,
  Of the mysteries above:
But I see that God hath spoken,
  How His well-belovèd Son
Kept the laws which man hath broken,
  Died for sins which man hath done.
Dying, rising, throned above!
'Now I see' that God is love.

Be not Weary.

Heb. xii. 2.

Yes! He knows the way is drea-ry, Knows the weak-ness of our frame, Knows that hand and heart are wea-ry— He 'in all points' felt the same. He is near to help and bless; Be not wea-ry, on-ward press.

Yes! He knows the way is dreary,
    Knows the weakness of our frame,
Knows that hand and heart are weary—
    He 'in all points" felt the same.
He is near to help and bless;
Be not weary, onward press.

Look to Him, who once was willing
    All His glory to resign;
That, for thee the law fulfilling,
    All His merit might be thine.
Strive to follow, day by day,
Where His footsteps mark the way.

Look to Him—the Lord of glory—
    Tasting death to win thy life;
Gazing on that 'wondrous story,'
    Canst thou falter in the strife?
Is it not new life to know
That the Lord hath loved thee so?

Look to Him—who ever liveth,
    Interceding for His own;
Seek, yea, claim, the grace He giveth
    Freely from His priestly throne:
Will He not thy strength renew,
With His Spirit's quickening dew?

Look to Him—and faith shall brighten,
    Hope shall soar, and love shall burn,
Peace once more thy heart shall lighten;
    Rise! He calleth thee: return!
Be not weary on thy way;
Jesus is thy strength and stay!

Not yet.

JOHN xiii. 7.

Not yet thou know-est what I do, O fee-ble child of earth,

Whose life is but to an-gel-view The morn-ing of thy birth.

The small-est leaf, the sim-plest flower, The wild bee's ho-ney cell,

Have les-sons of My love and power Too hard for thee to spell.

Not yet thou knowest what I do.
    O feeble child of earth,
Whose life is but to angel-view
    The morning of thy birth.
The smallest leaf, the simplest flower,
    The wild bee's honey cell,
Have lessons of My love and power
    Too hard for thee to spell.

Not yet thou knowest how I bid
    Each passing hour entwine
Its grief or joy, its hope or fear,
    In one great love-design ;
Nor how I lead thee through the night,
    By many a various way,
Still upward to unclouded light,
    And onward to the day.

Not yet thou knowest what I do
    Within thine own weak breast,
To mould thee to My image true,
    And fit thee for My rest.
But yield thee to My loving skill ;
    The veilèd work of grace,
From day to day progressing still,
    It is not thine to trace.

Yes, walk by faith and not by sight,
    Fast clinging to My hand ;
Content to feel My love and might—
    Not yet to understand.
A little while thy course pursue,
    Till grace to glory grow ;
Then what I am, and what I do,
    Hereafter thou shalt know.

Our Saviour and our King.

Heb. ii. 13.

Our Sa-viour and our King, En-throned and crowned a - bove,

Shall with ex - ceed - ing glad-ness bring The chil-dren of His love.

All that the Fa - ther gave, His glo - ry shall be - hold;

Not one whom Je - sus came to save Is miss-ing from His fold.

Our Saviour and our King,
   Enthroned and crowned above,
Shall with exceeding gladness bring
   The children of His love.
All that the Father gave,
   His glory shall behold;
Not one whom Jesus came to save
   Is missing from His fold.

He shall confess His own
   From every clime and coast,
Before His Father's glorious throne,
   Before the angel host.
'O righteous Father, see,
   In spotless robes arrayed,
Thy chosen gifts of love to Me,
   Before the worlds were made.

'By new creation Thine,
   By purpose and by grace,
By right of full redemption Mine,
   Faultless before Thy face.
As Thou hast lovèd Me,
   So hast Thou lovèd them;
Thy precious jewels they shall be,
   My glorious diadem!'

Now, and Afterward.

HEB. xii. 11.

p misterioso.

Now, the sow - ing and the weep - ing,

Work - ing hard and wait - ing long;

mf   *f*   *e poco cres.*

Af - ter - ward, the gold - en reap - ing,

Har - vest home and grate - ful song.

Now, the sowing and the weeping,
  Working hard and waiting long;
Afterward, the golden reaping,
  Harvest home and grateful song.

Now, the pruning, sharp, unsparing;
  Scattered blossom, bleeding shoot!
Afterward, the plenteous bearing
  Of the Master's pleasant fruit.

Now, the plunge, the briny burden,
  Blind, faint gropings in the sea;
Afterward, the pearly guerdon
  That shall make the diver free.

Now, the long and toilsome duty
  Stone by stone to carve and bring;
Afterward, the perfect beauty
  Of the palace of the King.

Now, the tuning and the tension,
  Wailing minors, discord strong;
Afterward, the grand ascension
  Of the Alleluia song.

Now, the spirit conflict-riven,
  Wounded heart, unequal strife;
Afterward, the triumph given,
  And the victor's crown of life.

Now, the training, strange and lowly,
  Unexplained and tedious now;
Afterward, the service holy,
  And the Master's 'Enter thou!'

The Things that are Behind.

Philip. iii. 13, 14.

Leave be - hind earth's emp - ty plea - sure,

Fleet - ing hope and chang - ing love ;

Leave its soon - - cor - ro - ding trea - sure,

There are bet - ter things a - bove.

Leave behind earth's empty pleasure,
    Fleeting hope and changing love;
Leave its soon-corroding treasure,
    There are better things above.

Leave, oh, leave thy fond aspirings,
    Bid thy restless heart be still;
Cease, oh, cease thy vain desirings,
    Only seek thy Father's will.

Leave behind thy faithless sorrow,
    And thine every anxious care;
He who only knows the morrow
    Can for thee its burden bear.

Leave behind the doubting spirit,
    And thy crushing load of sin;
By thy mighty Saviour's merit,
    Life eternal thou shalt win.

Leave the darkness gathering o'er thee,
    Leave the shadow-land behind;
Realms of glory lie before thee;
    Enter in and welcome find.

New Year.

Isa. xli. 10.

mf or f

Stand-ing at the por - tal, Of the op-'ning year, Words of com-fort

meet us, Hush-ing ev-'ry fear; Spo-ken thro' the si - lence,

cres.

By our Fa-ther's voice, Tender, strong, and faith - ful, Mak-ing us re - joice.

f CHORUS. *2nd time,* *ff*

On - ward then, and fear not, Chil - dren of the day!

For His word shall nev - er, Nev - er pass a - way.

Repeat Chorus, ff

Standing at the portal,
  Of the opening year,
Words of comfort meet us,
  Hushing every fear;
Spoken through the silence,
  By our Father's voice,
Tender, strong, and faithful,
  Making us rejoice.
    Onward then, and fear not,
      Children of the day!
    For His word shall never,
      Never pass away.

I, the Lord, am with thee,
  Be thou not afraid!
I will help and strengthen,
  Be thou not dismayed;
Yea, I will uphold thee
  With My own right hand,
Thou art called and chosen
  In My sight to stand.
    Onward then, &c.

For the year before us,
  Oh, what rich supplies!
For the poor and needy,
  Living streams shall rise;
For the sad and sinful
  Shall His grace abound;
For the faint and feeble,
  Perfect strength be found.
    Onward then, &c.

He will never fail us,
  He will not forsake;
His eternal covenant
  He will never break!
Resting on His promise,
  What have we to fear?
God is all-sufficient
  For the coming year!
    Onward then, and fear not,
      Children of the day!
    For His word shall never,
      Never pass away.

(33)

D

Hymn to the Holy Spirit.

Tune—"TRYPHOSA."   HEB. x. 15, 23.   *Music by* F. R. H.

To Thee,   O   Com - fort - er   Di - vine,

For   all   Thy   grace   and   power   be - nign,

Sing   we   Al - le - lu - ia!

Al - le - lu - ia!   Al - le - lu - ia!

To Thee, O Comforter Divine,
For all Thy grace and power benign,
    Sing we Alleluia!

To Thee, whose faithful love had place
In God's great Covenant of Grace,
    Sing we Alleluia!

To Thee, whose faithful voice doth win
The wandering from the ways of sin,
    Sing we Alleluia!

To Thee, whose faithful power doth heal,
Enlighten, sanctify, and seal,
    Sing we Alleluia!

To Thee, whose faithful truth is shown
By every promise made our own,
    Sing we Alleluia!

To Thee, our Teacher and our Friend,
Our faithful Leader to the end,
    Sing we Alleluia!

To Thee, by Jesus Christ sent down,
Of all His gifts the sum and crown,
    Sing we Alleluia!

To Thee, who art with God the Son
And God the Father ever One,
    Sing we Alleluia!

Alleluia!

HEB. x. 15, 23.

To Thee, O Com- fort - er Di - vine, For all Thy grace and power be - nign,

Sing we Al - le - lu - ia! To Thee, whose faith-ful love had place In

God's great Co - ve - nant of Grace, Sing we Al - le - lu - ia!

To Thee, whose faith-ful voice doth win The wan-d'ring from the ways of sin,

To Thee, O Comforter Divine,
For all Thy grace and power benign,
Sing we Alleluia!
To Thee, whose faithful love had place
In God's great Covenant of Grace,
Sing we Alleluia!
To Thee, whose faithful voice doth win
The wandering from the ways of sin,
Sing we Alleluia!
To Thee, whose faithful power doth heal,
Enlighten, sanctify, and seal,
Sing we Alleluia!

To Thee, whose faithful truth is shown,
By every promise made our own,
Sing we Alleluia!
To Thee, our Teacher and our Friend,
Our faithful Leader to the end,
Sing we Alleluia!
To Thee, by Jesus Christ sent down,
Of all His gifts the sum and crown,
Sing we Alleluia!
To Thee, who art with God the Son
And God the Father ever One,
Sing we Alleluia!

Is it for Me?

Cant. l. 7.

Is it for me, dear Sa - viour, Thy glo - ry and Thy rest?

For me, so weak and sin - ful, Oh, shall I thus be blest?

Is it for me to see Thee In all Thy glo - rious grace,

And gaze in end - less rap - ture On Thy be - lov - ed Face?

Is it for me, dear Saviour,
    Thy glory and Thy rest?
For me, so weak and sinful,
    Oh, shall I thus be blest?
Is it for me to see Thee
    In all Thy glorious grace,
And gaze in endless rapture
    On Thy belovèd Face?

Is it for me to listen
    To Thy belovèd Voice,
And hear its sweetest music,
    Bid even me rejoice?
Is it for me, Thy welcome,
    Thy gracious 'Enter in'?
For me, Thy ' Come, ye blessèd !'
    For me, so full of sin?

O Saviour, precious Saviour,
    My heart is at Thy feet,
I bless Thee and I love Thee,
    And Thee I long to meet.
A thrill of solemn gladness
    Has hushed my very heart,
To think that I shall really
    Behold Thee as Thou art;

Behold Thee in Thy beauty,
    Behold Thee face to face;
Behold Thee in Thy glory,
    And reap Thy smile of grace;
And be with Thee for ever,
    And never grieve Thee more !
Dear Saviour, I *must* praise Thee,
    And lovingly adore.

Spirituality of God.

JOHN iv. 24.

What know we, Ho - ly God, of Thee,

Thy be - ing and Thine es - sence pure?

Too bright the ve - ry mys - te - ry

For mor - tal vis - ion to en - dure.

What know we, Holy God, of Thee,
  Thy being and Thine essence pure ?
Too bright the very mystery
  For mortal vision to endure.

We only know Thy word sublime,
  Thou art a Spirit ! Perfect ! One !
Unlimited by space or time,
  Unknown but through the eternal Son.

By change untouched, by thought untraced,
  And by created eye unseen,
In *Thy great Present* is embraced
  All that shall be, all that hath been.

O Father of our spirits, now
  We seek Thee in our Saviour's face ;
In truth and spirit we would bow,
  And worship where we cannot trace.

Remembrance. (COMMUNION HYMN.)

Cant. ii. 3.

Sit down be - neath His sha - dow, And rest with great de - light;

The faith that now be - holds Him Is pledge of fu - ture sight.

Our Mas-ter's love re - mem - ber, Ex - ceed - ing great and free;

Lift up thy heart in glad - ness, For He re - mem-bers thee.

Sit down beneath His shadow,
And rest with great delight;
The faith that now beholds Him
Is pledge of future sight.
Our Master's love remember,
Exceeding great and free;
Lift up thy heart in gladness,
For He remembers thee.

Bring every weary burden,
Thy sin, thy fear, thy grief;
He calls the heavy laden
And gives them kind relief.
His righteousness 'all glorious'
Thy festal robe shall be;
And love that passeth knowledge
His banner over thee.

A little while, though parted,
Remember, wait, and love,
Until He comes in glory,
Until we meet above.
Till in the Father's kingdom
The heavenly feast is spread,
And we behold His beauty,
Whose blood for us was shed!

Wait Patiently for Him.

Ps. xxxvii. 7.

God doth not bid thee wait, To dis-ap-point at last;

A gold-en pro-mise, fair and great, In pre-cept-mould is cast.

Soon shall the morn-ing gild The dark ho-ri-zon rim,

Thy heart's de-sire shall be ful-filled, '*Wait* pa-tient-ly for Him.'

God doth not bid thee wait,
    To disappoint at last ;
A golden promise, fair and great,
    In precept-mould is cast.
Soon shall the morning gild
    The dark horizon rim,
Thy heart's desire shall be fulfilled,
    ' *Wait* patiently for Him.'

The weary waiting times
    Are but the muffled peals,
Low preluding celestial chimes
    That hail His chariot-wheels.
Trust Him to tune thy voice
    To blend with seraphim ;
His 'Wait' shall issue in 'Rejoice !'
    'Wait *patiently* for Him.'

He doth not bid thee wait,
    Like driftwood on the wave,
For fickle chance or fixèd fate
    To ruin or to save.
Thine eyes shall surely see,
    No distant hope or dim,
The Lord thy God arise for thee :
    'Wait patiently *for Him !*'

(45)

The Sovereignty of God.

Ps. xlvi. 10.

God Al- migh- ty! King of na- tions! earth Thy foot-stool, heaven Thy throne!

Thine the great-ness, power, and glo - ry, Thine the king-dom, Lord, a - lone!

Life and death are in Thy keep-ing, and Thy will or - dain-eth all:

From the ar- mies of Thy hea- vens to an un- seen in - sect's fall.

God Almighty! King of nations! earth Thy footstool, heaven Thy throne!

Thine the greatness, power, and glory, Thine the kingdom, Lord, alone!

Life and death are in Thy keeping, and Thy will ordaineth all :

From the armies of Thy heavens to an unseen insect's fall.

Reigning, guiding, all-commanding, ruling myriad worlds of light ;

Now exalting, now abasing, none can stay Thy hand of might !

Working all things by Thy power, by the counsel of Thy will,

Thou art God ! enough to know it, and to hear Thy word : ' Be still !'

In Thy sovereignty rejoicing, we Thy children bow and praise,

For we know that kind and loving, just and true are all Thy ways.

While Thy heart of sovereign mercy, and Thine arm of sovereign might,

For our great and strong salvation in Thy sovereign grace unite.

New Mercies.

REV. xxi. 5.

mf or f

New mer - cies, new bless - ings, new light on thy way;

New cou - rage, new hope, and new strength for each day;

New notes of thanks - giv - ing, new chords of de - light;

rall.

New praise in the morn - ing, new songs in the night;

New mercies, new blessings, new light on thy way;

New courage, new hope, and new strength for each day;

New notes of thanksgiving, new chords of delight;

New praise in the morning, new songs in the night;

New wine in thy chalice, new altars to raise;

New fruit for thy Master, new garments of praise;

New gifts from His treasures, new smiles from His face;

New streams from the Fountain of infinite grace;

New stars for thy crown, and new tokens of love;

New gleams of the glory that waits thee above;

New light of His countenance, clear and unpriced!

All this be the joy of thy new life in Christ!

This same Jesus.

ACTS i. 11.

'This same Je - sus!' oh! how sweet-ly   Fall those words up - on the ear,

Like   a   swell of   far - off   mu - sic   In   the night-watch still   and   drear.

He who healed the   hope - less   le - per,   He   who   dried   the   wi- dow's tear;

He who changed to health and glad- ness   Help-less   suf-f'ring, trem-bling fear.

'This same Jesus!' oh! how sweetly
  Fall those words upon the ear,
Like a swell of far-off music
  In the night-watch still and drear.
He who healed the hopeless leper,
  He who dried the widow's tear;
He who changed to health and gladness
  Helpless suff'ring, trembling fear.

He who wandered, poor and homeless,
  By the stormy Galilee;
He who on the night-robed mountain
  Bent in prayer the wearied knee;
He who spake as none had spoken,
  Angel-wisdom far above,
All-forgiving, ne'er upbraiding,
  Full of tenderness and love.

He who gently called the weary,
  'Come, and I will give you rest';
He who loved the little children,
  Took them in His arms and blest;
He, the lonely Man of Sorrows,
  'Neath our sin-curse bending low;
By His faithless friends forsaken
  In the darkest hour of woe.

He Himself, and 'not another,'
  He for whom our heart-love yearned
Through long years of twilight waiting,
  To His ransomed ones returned.
For His word, O Lord, we bless Thee,
  Bless our Master's changeless name;
Yesterday, to-day, for ever,
  Jesus Christ is still the same.

A Worker's Prayer.

ROM. xiv. 7.

Lord, speak to me, that I may speak In
liv - ing e - choes of Thy tone:
As Thou hast sought, so let me seek Thy
er - ring chil - dren, lost and lone.

Lord, speak to me, that I may speak
    In living echoes of Thy tone :
As Thou hast sought, so let me seek
    Thy erring children, lost and lone.

Oh, lead me, Lord, that I may lead
    The wandering and the wavering feet ;
Oh, feed me, Lord, that I may feed
    Thy hungering ones with manna sweet.

Oh, strengthen me, that while I stand
    Firm on the Rock, and strong in Thee,
I may stretch out a loving hand
    To wrestlers with the troubled sea.

Oh, teach me, Lord, that I may teach
    The precious things Thou dost impart ;
And wing my words, that they may reach
    The hidden depths of many a heart.

Oh, give Thine own sweet rest to me,
    That I may speak with soothing power
A word in season, as from Thee,
    To weary ones in needful hour.

Oh, fill me with Thy fulness, Lord,
    Until my very heart o'erflow
In kindling thought and glowing word,
    Thy love to tell, Thy praise to show.

Oh, use me, Lord, use even me,
    Just *as* Thou wilt, and *when*, and *where* ;
Until Thy blessèd Face I see,
    Thy rest, Thy joy, Thy glory share.

Our Commission.

Rev. xxii. 17.

mf

Ye   who   hear   the   bless - ed   call   Of   the

Spi - rit   and   the   Bride: Hear   the   Mas - ter's   word   to   all,

Your   com - mis - sion   and   your   guide—   'And   let

f

him   that   hear - eth   say,   Come,'   to   all   yet   far   a - way.

Ye who hear the blessèd call
 Of the Spirit and the Bride:
Hear the Master's word to all,
 Your commission and your guide—
'And let him that heareth say,
Come,' to all yet far away.

'Come!' alike to age and youth,
 Tell them of our Friend above,
Of His beauty and His truth,
 Preciousness and grace and love.
Tell them what you know is true,
Tell them what He is to you.

'Come!' to those who do not care
 For the Saviour's precious death,
Having not a thought to spare
 For the gracious words He saith.
Ere the shadows gather deep,
Rouse them from their fatal sleep.

'Come!' to those who, while they hear,
 Linger, hardly knowing why;
Tell them that the Lord is near,
 Tell them Jesus passes by.
Call them *now*; oh! do not wait,
Lest to-morrow be too late.

Brothers, sisters, do not wait,
 Speak for Him who speaks to you!
Wherefore should you hesitate?
 This is no great thing to do.
Jesus only bids you say,
'Come!' and will you not obey?

Lord! to Thy command we bow,
 Touch our lips with altar fire;
Let Thy Spirit kindle now
 Faith, and zeal, and strong desire;
So that henceforth we may be
Fellow-workers, Lord, with Thee!

Joined to Christ.

EPH. i. 22, 23.

Joined to Christ in mys-tic u-nion, We Thy mem-bers, Thou our Head, Sealed by deep and true com-mu-nion, Risen with Thee, who once were dead— Sa - viour, we would hum-bly claim All the power of this Thy name.

Joined to Christ in mystic union,
   We Thy members, Thou our Head,
Sealed by deep and true communion,
   Risen with Thee, who once were dead—
Saviour, we would humbly claim
All the power of this Thy name.

Instant sympathy to brighten
   All their weakness and their woe,
Guiding grace their way to lighten,
   Shall Thy loving members know;
All their sorrows Thou dost bear,
All Thy gladness they shall share.

Make Thy members every hour
   For Thy blessèd service meet ;
Earnest tongues, and arms of power,
   Skilful hands, and hastening feet,
Ever ready to fulfil
All Thy word and all Thy will.

Everlasting life Thou givest
   Everlasting love to see ;
They shall live because Thou livest,
   And their life is hid with Thee.
Safe Thy members shall be found,
When their glorious Head is crowned !

To Thee.

JOHN vi. 68.

I bring my sins to Thee, The sins I can-not count, That all may clean-sed be In Thy once o-pened Fount. I bring them, Sa-viour, all to Thee, The bur-den is too great for me.

I bring my sins to Thee,
  The sins I cannot count,
That all may cleansèd be
  In Thy once opened Fount.
I bring them, Saviour, all to Thee,
The burden is too great for me.

My heart to Thee I bring,
  The heart I cannot read ;
A faithless, wandering thing,
  An evil heart indeed.
I bring it, Saviour, now to Thee,
That fixed and faithful it may be.

To Thee I bring my care,
  The care I cannot flee,
Thou wilt not only share,
  But bear it all for me.
O loving Saviour, now to Thee
I bring the load that wearies me.

I bring my grief to Thee,
  The grief I cannot tell ;
No words shall needed be,
  Thou knowest all so well.
I bring the sorrow laid on me,
O suffering Saviour, now to Thee.

My joys to Thee I bring,
  The joys Thy love hath given,
That each may be a wing
  To lift me nearer heaven.
I bring them, Saviour, all to Thee,
For Thou hast purchased all for me.

My life I bring to Thee,
  I would not be my own ;
O Saviour, let me be
  Thine ever, Thine alone.
My heart, my life, my all I bring
To Thee, my Saviour and my King !

In Memoriam.

" Hermas."

Words by M. J. WALKER. Ps. lv. 23. *Music by* F. R. H.*

Je - sus, I will trust Thee, trust Thee with my soul;

Guil - ty, lost, and help - less, Thou can'st make me whole.

There is none in hea - ven or on earth like Thee:

Thou hast died for sin - ners— there - fore, Lord, for me.

* The first verse of this Hymn was sung by F. R. H. ten minutes before her glorious departure to " eternal rest "—June 3rd, 1879.

Jesus, I will trust Thee, trust Thee with my soul;
Guilty, lost, and helpless, Thou canst make me whole.
There is none in heaven or on earth like Thee:
Thou hast died for sinners—therefore, Lord, for me.

Jesus, I may trust Thee, name of matchless worth
Spoken by the angel at Thy wondrous birth;
Written, and for ever, on Thy cross of shame,
Sinners read and worship, trusting in that name.

Jesus, I must trust Thee, pondering Thy ways,
Full of love and mercy all Thine earthly days:
Sinners gathered round Thee, lepers sought Thy face—
None too vile or loathsome for a Saviour's grace.

Jesus, I can trust Thee, trust Thy written word,
Though Thy voice of pity I have never heard.
When Thy Spirit teacheth, to my taste how sweet—
Only may I hearken, sitting at Thy feet.

Jesus, I do trust Thee, trust without a doubt:
'Whosoever cometh, Thou wilt not cast out,'
Faithful is Thy promise, precious is Thy blood—
These my soul's salvation, Thou my Saviour God!—

Take my Life.

Tune—" PATMOS."*   2 SAM. xix. 30.   *Music by* CANON HAVERGAL.

Take my life, and let it be

Con - se - cra - ted, Lord, to Thee.

Take my mo - ments and my days,

Let them flow in cease - less praise.

* This setting of the late Canon Havergal's is included in this collection by F. R. H's. request.

Take my life, and let it be
Consecrated, Lord, to Thee.
Take my moments and my days,
Let them flow in ceaseless praise.

Take my hands, and let them move
With the impulse of Thy love.
Take my feet, and let them be
Swift and 'beautiful' for Thee.

Take my voice, and let me sing
Always, only, for my King.
Take my lips, and let them be
Filled with messages from Thee.

Take my silver and my gold,
Not a mite would I withhold.
Take my intellect, and use
Every power as Thou dost choose.

Take my will, and make it Thine !
It shall be no longer mine.
Take my heart, it is Thine own !
It shall be Thy royal throne.

Take my love, my Lord, I pour
At Thy feet its treasure-store.
Take myself, and I will be
Ever, only, all, for Thee.

Trusting.

ISA. xii. 2.

I am trust-ing Thee, Lord Je-sus, Trust-ing on-ly

Thee! Trust-ing Thee for full sal-va-tion, Great and free!

I am trust-ing Thee for par-don, At Thy feet I bow;

For Thy grace and ten-der mer-cy Trust-ing now.

I am trusting Thee, Lord Jesus,
   Trusting only Thee !
Trusting Thee for full salvation,
   Great and free !
I am trusting Thee for pardon,
   At Thy feet I bow ;
For Thy grace and tender mercy
   Trusting now.

I am trusting Thee for cleansing
   In the crimson flood ;
Trusting Thee to make me holy,
   By Thy blood.
I am trusting Thee to guide me,
   Thou alone shalt lead,
Every day and hour supplying
   All my need.

I am trusting Thee for power ;
   Thine can never fail :
Words which Thou Thyself shalt give me
   Must prevail.
I am trusting Thee, Lord Jesus,
   Never let me fall !
I am trusting Thee for ever,
   And for all.

Our King.

Tune—"ZOAN."*   Ps. xlv. 11.   *Music by* CANON HAVERGAL.

O Sa - viour, pre - cious Sa - viour, Whom yet un-seen we love,

O Name of might and fa - vour, All o - ther names a - bove:

We wor - ship Thee, we bless Thee, To Thee a - lone we sing;

We praise Thee, and con - fess Thee Our ho - ly Lord and King!

* This setting also of Canon Havergal's to these words is included by F. R. H's. express desire.

O Saviour, precious Saviour,
  Whom yet unseen we love,
O Name of might and favour,
  All other names above :
      We worship Thee, we bless Thee,
        To Thee alone we sing ;
      We praise Thee, and confess Thee
        Our holy Lord and King !

O Bringer of salvation,
  Who wondrously hast wrought,
Thyself the revelation
  Of love beyond our thought :
      We worship Thee, we bless Thee,
        To Thee alone we sing ;
      We praise Thee, and confess Thee
        Our gracious Lord and King !

In Thee all fulness dwelleth,
  All grace and power divine ;
The glory that excelleth,
  O Son of God, is Thine :
      We worship Thee, we bless Thee,
        To Thee alone we sing ;
      We praise Thee, and confess Thee
        Our glorious Lord and King !

Oh, grant the consummation
  Of this our song above,
In endless adoration,
  And everlasting love :
      Then shall we praise and bless Thee,
        Where perfect praises ring,
      And evermore confess Thee
        Our Saviour and our King !

A Question to All.

Ps. li. 15.

Have you not a word for Je-sus? not a word to say for Him?

He is list-'ning thro' the cho-rus of the burn-ing se-ra-phim!

He is list-'ning: does He hear you speak-ing of the things of earth,

On - ly of its pass-ing plea-sure, sel - fish sor - row, emp-ty mirth?

Part I.

Have you not a word for Jesus? not a word to say for Him?
He is listening through the chorus of the burning seraphim!
He is listening: does He hear you speaking of the things of earth,
Only of its passing pleasure, selfish sorrow, empty mirth?

He has spoken words of blessing, pardon, peace, and love to you,
Glorious hopes and gracious comfort, strong and tender, sweet and true;
Does He hear you telling others something of His love untold,
Overflowings of thanksgiving for His mercies manifold?

Have you not a word for Jesus? Will the world His praise proclaim?
Who shall speak if ye are silent, ye who know and love His name?
You, whom He hath called and chosen His own witnesses to be,
Will you tell your gracious Master, 'Lord, we cannot speak for Thee!'

'Cannot!' though He suffered for you, died because He loved you so!
'Cannot!' though He has forgiven, making scarlet white as snow!
'Cannot!' though His grace abounding is your freely promised aid!
'Cannot!' though He stands beside you, though He says, 'Be not afraid!'

What shall be our word for Jesus? Master, give it day by day,
Ever as the need arises, teach Thy children what to say.
Give us holy love and patience, grant us deep humility,
That of self we may be emptied, and our hearts be full of Thee.

Part II.

Yes, we have a word for Jesus! Living echoes we will be
Of Thine own sweet words of blessing, of Thy gracious 'Come to Me!'
Jesus, Master! yes, we love Thee! and to prove our love would lay
Fruit of lips which Thou wilt open, at Thy blessèd feet to-day.

Give us grace to follow fully, vanquishing our faithless shame,
Feebly it may be, but truly, witnessing for Thy dear name.
Ours shall be the joy and honour Thy redeemèd ones to bring,
Jewels for the coronation of our coming Lord and King.

Yes, we have a word for Jesus! We will bravely speak for Thee;
And Thy bold and faithful soldiers, Saviour, we would henceforth be;
In Thy name set up our banners, while Thine own shall wave above,
With Thy crimson Name of Mercy, and Thy golden Name of Love.

Help us lovingly to labour, looking for Thy present smile,
Looking for Thy promised blessing, through the brightening 'little while.'
Words for Thee in weakness spoken Thou wilt here accept and own,
And confess them in Thy glory, when we see Thee on Thy throne.

The Ministry of Song.*

PROV. x. 16; 1 COR. xiv. 15.

In God's great field of la-bour All work is not the same;

He hath a ser-vice for each one Who loves His ho-ly name;

And you to whom the se-crets Of all sweet sounds are known,

Rise up! for He hath called you To a mis-sion of your own.

* Suitable for " Services of Song."

(70)

And right - ly to ful - fil it His grace will make you strong,

Who to your charge hath gi - ven The min - is - try of song.

In God's great field of labour
  All work is not the same ;
He hath a service for each one
  Who loves His holy name ;
And you to whom the secrets
  Of all sweet sounds are known,
Rise up ! for He hath called you
  To a mission of your own.
And rightly to fulfil it
  His grace will make you strong,
Who to your charge hath given
  The ministry of song.

Sing on in grateful gladness,
  Rejoice in this good thing,
Which the Lord thy God hath given
    to thee :
  The happy power to sing ;
But yield to Him, the Sovereign
  To whom all gifts belong,
In fullest consecration,
  Your ministry of song ;
Until His mercy grant you
  That resurrection voice,
Whose only ministry shall be
  To praise Him and rejoice.

Thee Alone.

JOHN xv. 5.

I could not do with-out Thee, O. Sa-viour of the lost!

Whose pre-cious blood re-deemed me At such tre-men-dous cost.

Thy righ-teous-ness, Thy par-don, Thy pre-cious blood must be

My on-ly hope and com-fort, My glo-ry and my plea.

I could not do without Thee,
    O Saviour of the lost !
Whose precious blood redeemed me
    At such tremendous cost.
Thy righteousness, Thy pardon,
    Thy precious blood must be
My only hope and comfort,
    My glory and my plea.

I could not do without Thee !
    I cannot stand alone ;
I have no strength or goodness,
    No wisdom of my own.
But Thou, belovèd Saviour,
    Art all in all to me ;
And weakness will be power,
    If leaning hard on Thee.

I could not do without Thee !
    For oh ! the way is long,
And I am often weary,
    And sigh replaces song.
How *could* I do without Thee ?
    I do not know the way ;
Thou knowest and Thou leadest,
    And wilt not let me stray.

I could not do without Thee,
    O Jesus, Saviour dear !
E'en when my eyes are holden,
    I know that Thou art near.
How dreary and how lonely
    This changeful life would be,
Without the sweet communion,
    The secret rest with Thee.

I could not do without Thee !
    No other friend can read
The spirit's strange deep longings,
    Interpreting its need.
No human heart could enter
    Each dim recess of mine,
And soothe and hush and calm it,
    O blessed Lord, but Thine !

I could not do without Thee !
    For years are fleeting fast,
And soon, in solemn loneliness,
    The river must be passed.
But Thou wilt never leave me,
    And though the waves roll high,
I know Thou wilt be near me,
    And whisper, ' It is I.'

Second Advent.

2 THESS. ii. 1.

Thou art com-ing, O my Sa-viour! Thou art com-ing, O my King!

In Thy beau-ty all - resplendent, In Thy glo-ry all-transcendent; Well may we re -

- joice and sing! Com-ing! In the op-'ning east, Her-ald brightness slow - ly swells!

Com-ing! O my glo-rious Priest, Hear we not Thy gold - en bells?

Thou art coming, O my Saviour!
/ Thou art coming, O my King!
In Thy beauty all-resplendent,
In Thy glory all-transcendent;
    Well may we rejoice and sing!
Coming! In the opening east,
    Herald brightness slowly swells!
Coming! O my glorious Priest,
    Hear we not Thy golden bells?

Thou art coming! Thou art coming!
    We shall meet Thee on Thy way,
We shall see Thee, we shall know
        Thee,   [Thee
We shall bless Thee, we shall show
    All our hearts could never say!
What an anthem that will be,
    Ringing out our love to Thee,
Pouring out our rapture sweet
    At Thine own all-glorious feet!

Thou art coming! Rays of glory
    Through the veil Thy death has
        rent,
Touch the mountain and the river
With a golden, glowing quiver,
    Thrill of light and music blent.
Earth is brightened when this gleam
    Falls on flower, and rock, and
        stream;
Life is brightened when this ray
    Falls upon its darkest day.

Thou art coming! We are waiting
    With a hope that cannot fail;
Asking not the day or hour,
Resting on Thy word of power
    Anchored safe within the veil.

Time appointed may be long,
    But the vision must be sure:
Certainty shall make us strong,
    Joyful patience can endure!

Oh the joy to see Thee reigning,
    Thee, my own belovèd Lord!
Every tongue Thy name confessing,
Worship, honour, glory, blessing,
    Brought to Thee with glad ac-
        cord!
Thee, my Master and my Friend,
    Vindicated and enthroned;
Unto earth's remotest end
    Glorified, adored, and owned!

Not a cloud and not a shadow,
    Not a mist and not a tear,
Not a sin and not a sorrow,
Not a dim and veiled to-morrow,
    For that sunrise grand and clear!
Jesus, Saviour, once with Thee,
    Nothing else seems worth a
        thought!
Oh how marvellous will be
    All the bliss Thy pain hath bought

Thou art coming! At Thy table
    We are witnesses for this,
While remembering hearts Thou
        meetest,
In communion clearest, sweetest,
    Earnest of our coming bliss.
Showing not Thy death alone,
    And Thy love exceeding great,
But Thy coming and Thy throne,
    All for which we long and wait.

Birthday or Anniversary.

Exod. iii. 12.

mp or mf

' Cer - tain - ly I will be with thee !' Fa - ther, I have found it true :

To Thy faith-ful-ness and mer - cy I would set my seal a - new.

All the year Thy grace hath kept me, Thou my help in-deed hast been,

Mar - vel - lous the lov-ing-kind-ness ev-'ry day and hour hath seen.

'Certainly I will be with thee!' Father, I have found it true:
To Thy faithfulness and mercy I would set my seal anew.
All the year Thy grace hath kept me, Thou my help indeed hast been,
Marvellous the lovingkindness every day and hour hath seen.

'Certainly I will be with thee!' Let me feel it, Saviour dear,
Let me know that Thou art with me, very precious, very near.
On this day of solemn pausing, with Thyself all longing still,
Let Thy pardon, let Thy presence, let Thy peace my spirit fill.

'Certainly I will be with thee!' Blessèd Spirit, come to me,
Rest upon me, dwell within me, let my heart Thy temple be;
Through the trackless year before me, Holy One, with me abide!
Teach me, comfort me, and calm me, be my ever-present Guide.

'Certainly I will be with thee!' Starry promise in the night!
All uncertainties, like shadows, flee away before its light.
'Certainly I will be with thee!' He hath spoken: I have heard!
True of old, and true this moment, I will trust Jehovah's word.

BY THE SAME AUTHOR.

ROYAL GRACE AND LOYAL GIFTS.

The following six volumes, 16mo, cloth, in elegant case, price 8s. 6d. These volumes may be had separately, price 1s. each.

KEPT FOR THE MASTER'S USE.

THE ROYAL INVITATION ; or, Daily Thoughts on Coming to Christ.

LOYAL RESPONSES ; or, Daily Melodies for the King's Minstrels.

ROYAL COMMANDMENTS ; or, Morning Thoughts for the King's Servants.

ROYAL BOUNTY ; or, Evening Thoughts for the King's Guests.

MY KING ; or, Daily Thoughts for the King's Children.

Just published, Royal 32mo, 9d. cloth.
MORNING STARS ; or, Names of Christ for His Little Ones.

Royal 32mo, each 6d. ; sewed, 9d. cloth.
MORNING BELLS AND LITTLE PILLOWS. Being Waking and Good-Night Thoughts for the Little Ones.

LONDON : JAMES NISBET & CO., 21, BERNERS STREET.

BY THE SAME AUTHOR.

Post 4to, in extra cloth gilt, 12s.   Bound by Burn.

LIFE MOSAIC: "The Ministry of Song" and "Under the Surface" in one volume. By FRANCES R. HAVERGAL. With twelve illustrations of Alpine scenery and flowers, by the Baroness HELGA VON CRAMM. Printed, in colours, under the superintendence of the Artist, by KAUFMANN, of Baden.

Foolscap 4to, 3s. cloth, gilt edges, or in paper covers, 1s. 6d.

SONGS OF PEACE AND JOY. The Words selected from "The Ministry of Song," and "Under the Surface." By FRANCES RIDLEY HAVERGAL. The Music by CHARLES H. PURDAY.

Royal 32mo, 1s. 6d. cloth, gilt edges.

THE MINISTRY OF SONG.

Crown 8vo, 5s. cloth ;
also Cheap Edition, royal 32mo, gilt edges, 1s. 6d. cloth.

UNDER THE SURFACE, and other Poems.

Small Crown 8vo, 3s. 6d. cloth ; also Cheap Editions, 1s. sewed, and 1s. 6d. cloth limp.

BRUEY. A Little Worker for Christ.

Royal 16mo, 1s. cloth.

THE FOUR HAPPY DAYS.

LONDON : JAMES NISBET & CO., 21, BERNERS STREET.

MEMORIALS OF THE AUTHOR, &c.

Just published, demy 8vo, 1s.

FRANCES RIDLEY HAVERGAL MEMORIAL CARD. Designed by the Baroness HELGA VON CRAMM, and exquisitely printed in Oil Colours by KAUFMANN, of Baden.

Imperial 32mo, 2d. sewed, 6d. cloth.

MEMORIAL of THE LATE FRANCES RIDLEY HAVERGAL. " The Last Week."

HAVERGAL'S PSALMODY AND CENTURY OF CHANTS.

A.   6s. 6d.   D.   3s. 6d.

Without Chants.   B.   5s.   E.   3s.   Paper Covers, 2s. 3d.

Four Additional Tunes (Nos. 254—257).   Price 2d.

A Selection of 100 Tunes from the above, suited to Mission Services and Children's Songs of Grace and Glory.   Price 4d.   Cloth limp, 6d.

N.B.—A valuable Appendix, of 69 Hymns, suited to the special requirements of the present day, may be had bound up with any of the above, for 6d. extra, except P, with which it will be 3d. extra, and F, G, N, and O, with which it will be 4d. extra.

LONDON : JAMES NISBET & CO., 21, BERNERS STREET.

Index to First Lines of *Songs of Peace and Joy*

Thy Word, O Lord

"Thy word is a lamp unto my feet, and a light unto my path."   Psa. 119, 105.

Sandon. 10.4.10.4.10.10.

To be sung brightly.

Words by Albert Midlane
Music by Charles Henry Purday

Thy Word, O Lord, Thy pre-cious Word a-lone, Can lead me
By this, un - til The dark-some night be - gone, Lead Thou me

on ; Thy Word is light, Thy Word is life and pow'r, By
on ;

it, O guide me in each try - ing hour!

2. This all I have; around no light appears,
     O lead me on!
With eyes on Thee, though gazing through my tears,
     Lead Thou me on!
The good and best might lead me far astray,
Omniscient Saviour, lead Thou me, I pray!

3. Whate'er my path, led by Thy Word, 'tis good;
     O lead me on!
Be my poor heart Thy blessed Word's abode,
     Lead Thou me on!
Thy Holy Spirit gives the light to see,
And leads me, by Thy Word, close following Thee!

4. Led by aught else, I tread a devious way:
     O lead me on!
Speak, Lord, and help me ever to obey,
     Lead Thou me on!
My every step shall then be well defined,
And all I do according to Thy mind!

Albert Midlane (1825–1909)

Like a River Glorious

"Thou wilt keep him in perfect peace whose mind is stayed on thee." Isa. 26, 3.

Wye Valley. 6.5. (12 lines).

Words by Frances Ridley Havergal
Music by James Mountain

Like a ri-ver glo-rious Is God's per-fect peace, O-ver all vic-

to-rious In its bright in-crease. Per-fect— yet it flo-weth Ful-ler e-v'ry

day; Per-fect—yet it grow-eth Deeper all the way.

Chorus

Stayed u-pon Je-ho-vah, Hearts are ful-ly blest, Fin-ding, as He pro-mised, Per-fect peace and rest.

2. Hidden in the hollow
    Of His blessèd hand,
  Never foe can follow,
    Never traitor stand.
  Not a surge of worry,
    Not a shade of care,
  Not a blast of hurry
    Touch the spirit there.
      Chorus. Stayed upon Jehovah, . . . etc.

3. Every joy or trial
    Falleth from above,
  Traced upon our dial
    By the Sun of Love.
  We may trust Him solely
    All for us to do;
  They who trust Him wholly,
    Find Him wholly true.
      Chorus. Stayed upon Jehovah, . . . etc.

Frances Ridley Havergal
Twenty-fifth Day of *Loyal Responses*

Resting

"This is the rest wherewith ye may cause the weary to rest ; and this is the refreshing." Isaiah 28, 12.

Resting. 11.11.11.11.

Joyful.

Words by Frances Ridley Havergal
Music by James Mountain

2. Resting 'neath His guiding hand for untracked days;
Resting 'neath His shadow from the noontide rays;
Resting at the eventide beneath His wing,
In the fair pavilion of our Saviour King.

3. Resting in the fortress while the foe is nigh;
Resting in the lifeboat while the waves roll high;
Resting in His chariot for the swift glad race;
Resting, always resting in His boundless grace.

4. Resting in the pastures, and beneath the Rock;
Resting by the waters where He leads His flock;
Resting, while we listen, at His glorious feet;
Resting in His very arms!—O rest complete!

5. Resting and believing, let us onward press,
Resting in Himself, the Lord our Righteousness;
Resting and rejoicing, let His saved ones sing,
Glory, glory, glory be to Christ our King.

Frances Ridley Havergal
Sixteenth Day of *Loyal Responses*

Jesus Christ, the Crucified

Words by Johann C. Schwedler
Music by Henri Abraham César Malan, harmonized by Lowell Mason

Hendon

Ask ye what great thing I know, That de - lights and stirs me so? What the high re - ward I win? Whose the Name I glo - ry in? Je - sus Christ, the Cru - ci - fied.

2. What is faith's foundation strong?
What awakes my heart to song?
He Who bore my sinful load,
Purchased for me peace with God,
   Jesus Christ, the Crucified.

3. Who is He that makes me wise
To discern where duty lies?
Who is He that makes me true
Duty, when discerned to do,
   Jesus Christ, the Crucified.

4. Who defeats my fiercest foes?
Who consoles my saddest woes?
Who revives my fainting heart,
Healing all its hidden smart?
   Jesus Christ, the Crucified.

5. Who is life in life to me?
Who the death of death will be?
Who will place me on His right,
With the countless hosts of light?
   Jesus Christ, the Crucified.

6. This is that great thing I know;
This delights and stirs me so;
Faith in Him Who died to save,
Him Who triumphed o'er the grave:
   Jesus Christ, the Crucified.

This is sung to Malan's "Hendon," the same score that is widely sung for the Consecration Hymn in the United States.

Luke 9:13.

The Lord commanded, "Give ye them to eat,"—
    Five loaves and two small fishes all their store
    For hungering crowds. He knew they had no more,
And He had called them to that wild retreat.
They gave it as He gave them, piece by piece,
    Where on the green grass grouped the great and small
    Till all were filled. So not theirs at all
But His, the glory of that grand increase.
Master, I have not strength to serve Thee much,
    The "half-day's work" is all that I can do,
But let Thy mighty, multiplying touch
    Even to me the miracle renew.
Let five words feed five thousand, and Thy power
Expand to life-results one feeble hour.

Song.   F.R.H. (date not known)

There is music by the river,
    And music by the sea,
And music in the waterfall
    That gusheth glad and free.
There is music in the brooklet
    That singeth all alone,
There is music in the fountain
    With its silver-tinkling tone.

But the music of thy spirit
    Is sweeter far to me
Than the melody of rivers,
    Or the anthems of the sea.
Why should I dwell in silence
    When the music is so near
That may overflow my spirit
        So full, so clear!
            Oh! let me listen!

There is music in the forest,
    A myriad-voicèd song;
And music on the mountains
    As the great winds rush along:
There is music in the gladness
    Of morning's merry light,
And in silence of the noontide,
    And in hush of starry night.

But a deeper, holier music
    Is the music of thy soul,
And I think the angels listen
    As its starry echoes roll.
Why should I dwell in silence
    When the music that is thine
May overflow my spirit
        And blend—with mine!
            Oh! let me listen!
        F.R.H. January 16, 1874

A Silence and a Song.

I am alone, dear Master—
    Alone in heart with Thee!
Though merry faces round me
    And loving looks I see.

There's a hush among the blithe ones,
    While a pleasant voice is heard,
A truce to all the tournament
    Of flashing wit and word.

And in that truce of silence,
    I lay aside my lance,
And through the light and music send
    One happy upward glance.

I know not what the song may be,
    The words I cannot hear;
'Tis but a gentle melody,
    All simple, soft, and clear.

But the sweetness and the quiet
    Have set my spirit free,
And I turn in loving gladness,
    Dear Master, now to Thee.

I know I love Thee better
    Than any earthly joy,
For Thou hast given me the peace
    Which nothing can destroy.

I know that Thou art nearer still
    Than all this merry throng,
And sweeter is the thought of Thee
    Than any lovely song.

The Song Chalice.

"You bear the chalice." Is it so, my friend?
    Have I indeed a chalice of sweet song,
    With underflow of harmony made strong
New calm of strength through throbbing veins to send?
I did not form or fill,—I do but spend
    That which the Master poured into my soul,
    His dewdrops caught in a poor earthen bowl,
That service so with praise might meekly blend.
May He who taught the morning stars to sing,
    Aye keep my chalice cool, and pure, and sweet,
And grant me so with loving hand to bring
    Refreshment to His weary ones,—to meet
Their thirst with water from God's music-spring;
    And, bearing thus, to pour it at His feet.

                F.R.H. January 7, 1869

Thou hast put gladness in my heart,
    Then well may I be glad!
Without the secret of Thy love,
    I could not but be sad.

I bless Thee for these pleasant hours
    With sunny-hearted friends,
But more for this sweet moment's calm
    Thy loving-kindness sends.

O Master, gracious Master,
    What will Thy presence be,
If such a thrill of joy can crown
    One upward look to Thee?

'Tis ending now, that gentle song,
    And they will call for me;
They know the music I love best,—
    My song shall be for Thee!

For Thee, who hast so lovèd us,
    And whom, not having seen,
We love; on whom in all our joy,
    As in our grief, we lean.

Be near me still, and tune my notes,
    And make them sweet and strong,
To waft Thy words to many a heart
    Upon the wings of song.

I know that all will listen,
    For my very heart shall sing,
And it shall be Thy praise alone,
    My glorious Lord and King.

                F.R.H. March 16, 1871